DUSTIN PEDROIA

Joe Gaspar

PowerKiDS press

New York

Published in 2011 by The Rosen Publishing Group, Inc.
29 East 21st Street, New York, NY 10010

First Edition

Editor: Amelie von Zumbusch
Book Design: Kate Laczynski
Photo Researcher: Jessica Gerweck

Photo Credits: Cover, p. 1 G. Fiume/Getty Images; p. 4 Jamie Squire/ Getty Images; pp. 7, 19 Rich Pilling/MLB Photos via Getty Images; p. 8 Elsa/Getty Images; p. 11 Otto Greule Jr/Getty Images; p. 12 Brad Mangin/MLB Photos via Getty Images; p. 15 Jed Jacobsin/Getty Images; p. 16 Christian Petersen/Getty Images; p. 20 Jeff Gross/Getty Images; p. 22 G. Newman Lowrance/ Getty Images.

Library of Congress Cataloging-in-Publication Data

Gaspar, Joe.
  Dustin Pedroia / Joe Gaspar. — 1st ed.
     p. cm. — (Baseball's mvps)
  Includes index.
  ISBN 978-1-4488-0630-0 (library binding) —
  ISBN 978-1-4488-1784-9 (pbk.) — ISBN 978-1-4488-1785-6 (6-pack)
  1. Pedroia, Dustin. 2. Baseball players—United States—Biography.
  I. Title.
  GV865.P43G37 2011
  796.357092—dc22
  [B]
                     2009045772

Manufactured in the United States of America

CPSIA Compliance Information: Batch #WS10PK: For Further Information contact Rosen Publishing, New York, New York at 1-800-237-9932

CONTENTS

4

Dustin Pedroia is a baseball player. He was born in Woodland, California.

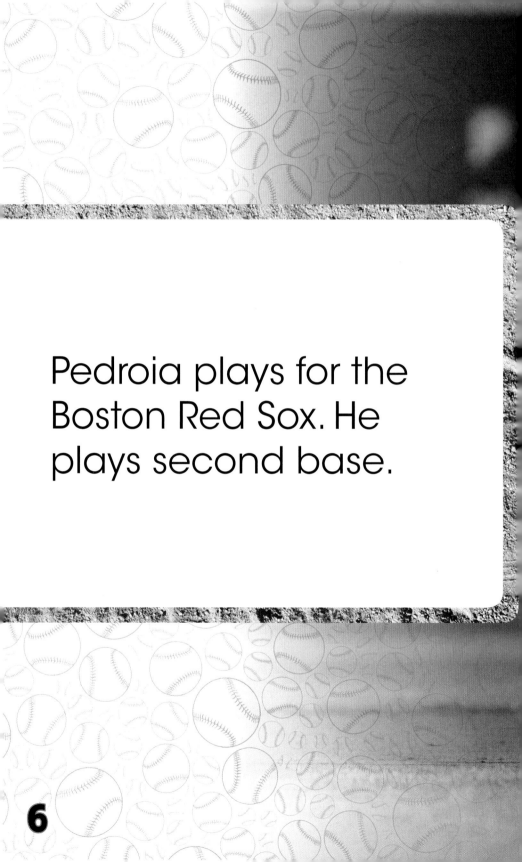

Pedroia plays for the Boston Red Sox. He plays second base.

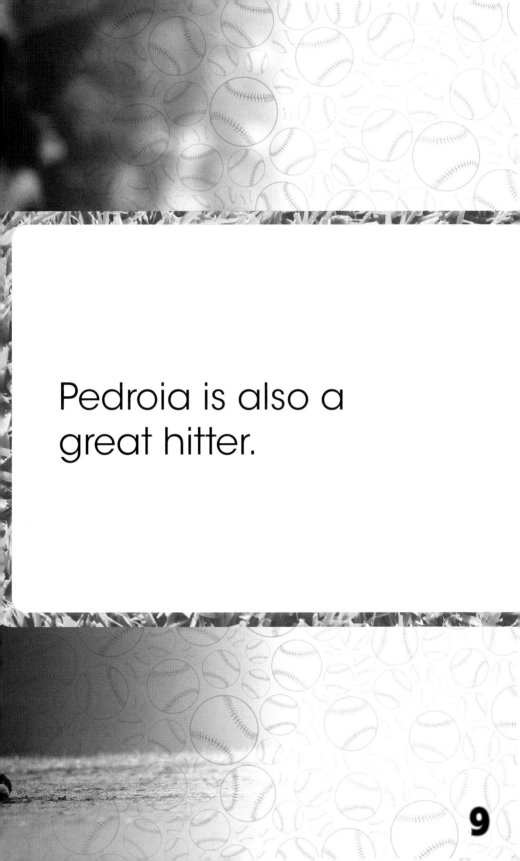

Pedroia is also a great hitter.

Pedroia started
playing for the Red
Sox in 2006.

Pedroia's first full year with the Red Sox was 2007.

Pedroia played very well in 2007. He was named **Rookie** of the Year.

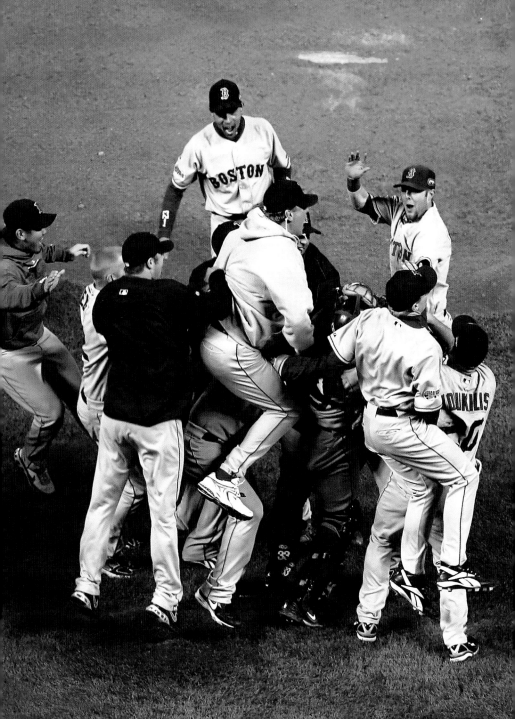

Pedroia helped the Red Sox win the 2007 **World Series**.

The next year, Pedroia played even better. He hit 17 home runs!

19

Pedroia was the American **League** MVP, or most **valuable** player, in 2008.

Today, Pedroia is one of the Red Sox's biggest stars.

Here are more books to read about Dustin Pedroia and baseball:

Connery-Boyd, Peg. *Red Sox Coloring and Activity Book*. 3rd Ed. Mystic, CT: Hawk's Nest Publishing, LLC, 2009.

Stewart, Mark. *The Boston Red Sox*. Team Spirit Book. Chicago: Norwood House Press, 2008.

Due to the changing nature of Internet links, PowerKids Press has developed an online list of Web sites related to the subject of this book. This site is updated regularly. Please use this link to access the list:
www.powerkidslinks.com/bmvp/dp/

GLOSSARY

league (LEEG) A group of sports teams.

rookie (RU-kee) A new major-league player.

valuable (VAL-yoo-bul) Important.

World Series (WURLD SEER-eez) A group of games in which the two best baseball teams play against each other.

INDEX